How To Grow Citrus Practically Anywhere

By: Darren Sheriff

a.k.a The Citrus Guy

Copyright © 2016 The Citrus Guy

All rights reserved.

ISBN: **1530654106**
ISBN-13: **978-1530654109**

DEDICATION

I would like to dedicate this book to my wife Tammy and my mother Dee. My wife for encouraging me to buy that poor little Calamondin tree that started this whole Citrus mess. My mother for teaching me and showing me how to garden and deal with plants.
I Love You Both!

Darren Sheriff a.k.a The Citrus Guy

How To Grow Citrus Practically Anywhere

Me, at the 2015 Citrus Expo

This is a lecture inside of a book.

A compilation of information learned and given during the many lectures I have done and from FAQ's that The Citrus Guy has entertained since 2007 when I started conducting my talks.

PREFACE:

As I was writing this book, I had every intention of making it more of a Textbook of sorts. As it progressed, it became more of how I would give one of my lectures to a garden club, complete with pictures. I have been speaking on growing citrus since 2007, I actually started learning and growing them back in 1998. My very first citrus tree was a calamondin. I always include the story on how that tree came into my life, at some point, during my lectures.

It basically goes like this.

My wife and I were at a grocery store, just after Christmas. We were walking past the floral department and there was this poor little calamondin, sitting on the counter, 50% off.

It was a sad, pathetic looking little thing. It had a couple of fruits on it and just needed some TLC. My wife told me I should buy it. At the time I had no interest in growing any kind of citrus, never even crossed my mind. I told her, no, I don't think so. She insisted that I should and I kept telling her no. Well, she finally prevailed and now, she regrets those words. I joke about that last part actually she loves the fresh fruit.

My second tree was a Key Lime. I honestly do not know what happened after that one!!

At one time, and this is the honest truth, I had 119 different cultivars of citrus, all in containers, in our yard. I am not just talking about 119 citrus trees, the actual count was something like 127, I am talking 119 ACTUAL differently, named, and tasting citrus cultivars/varieties. Due to some financial situations and my newfound love of Camellias, I whittled that down, at the time of this writing, to some 65 or so cultivars.

Now, now, don't judge me, I needed the room for the Camellias. I use them to sooth my competitive nature. But that is getting off topic and probably will be one of my next books.

I should also mention that, the number 65 will probably not last long. I am always looking for something new, different or unique in the citrus world. I actually just planted a bunch of different blood type citrus, blood oranges, blood limes, etc. I hope to someday hybridize a blood kumquat. That will definitely be down the road however.

When I became a Master Gardener back in 2007, they hung "The Citrus Guy" name on me and I will probably, forever have that name here in Charleston. I have a friend, named Stan McKenzie. He will always be known as "Stan, The Citrus Man". I have learned a lot from him as well as many other "Citruholics". Hopefully, I will repay many of them back with my references to websites, nurseries and what have you as this book unfolds.

Thanks Guys!! (And Gals)

How To Grow Citrus Practically Anywhere

CHAPTER 1: INTRODUCTION

Citrus.

The word itself conjures up pictures of huge groves in Florida. Maybe you think about that first morning glass of orange juice or a grapefruit cut in half as a snack.

I understand, not everybody can move to Florida or California, but wouldn't you love to live in a place that, just outside your back door, is a tree that you can pick your own fresh citrus fruit?

This book will help you do just that!

"How to grow citrus practically anywhere" is designed to help people, who are not exactly living in prime citrus producing areas.

This book will not go into how to grow them in the ground, if you are in a place warm enough to grow it that way, there are plenty of other books out there for that. This is going to be more on container cultivation. This book will be beneficial if you have say, a large patio that you can't plant a tree into the ground. A balcony in the city might confront you. Maybe you rent and one day will want to move, you can take them with you. Perhaps, you like to rearrange furniture or the knick-knacks in the house; wouldn't it be fun to do that in your yard? Probably one of the main reasons you will want to read this book is if you live in a very cold place, Maine comes to mind. There are not too many tangerines being produced up there! But there could be. As long as you have a sunny, warm room, a greenhouse or a place to hang some lights and the desire to put some real effort into it, you can grow Calamondins in Canada and Mandarins in Massachusetts.

How is THAT for optimism?

Growing citrus in containers is no harder than growing any other plant. Yes, it can get big and, I will not kid you, there is a great deal of work involved. As Thomas Edison once said, "The three great essentials to achieve anything worth while are: Hard Work, Stick-to-itiveness, and Common Sense".

This book is going to help you with all three of those.

Chapter 2 will start out with a little history on citrus. It is always nice to know where something comes from. Where it has been or how it got someplace else. By researching the origins, this also gives you a better idea of what kind of growing conditions it is accustomed to.

Chapter 3 will be all about what to search out to grow. This chapter will give you examples of the different cultivars as well as the different citrus fruits out there. Taste is so different among people; it would be impossible to describe what each tastes like. I will give you a list of what I know is good, what some of the odd things are used for, and give you an idea of what to start with.

Chapter 4 will discuss your trees home. What size pot to use, when to repot. It will give you the benefits, pro and con, to using plastic versus terracotta and other materials.

Chapter 5 will tell you what to fill those pots up with. Soil is the basis for which your plants survive. What are some of the best and worst out there, what are some of the different combinations of ingredients that can be used, why some are better than others, etc.

Chapter 6 is all about fertilizers. What to use, what to avoid and what kinds of things happen to fertilizers over a period of time. What the purpose of using fertilizers is, good and bad. It will also discuss deficiencies, what to look for in your tree and how to correct them.

Chapter 7 will be on watering and sunlight, you would think that these would be two things that are easy to supply! In containers it actually gets a little tricky. Too much sun is just as bad as too little. Water can be an enemy for a couple of reasons.

Chapter 8 really gets to the heart of the matter, protection. This is the main reason that it is difficult to grow citrus above a Zone 8. In this chapter we will discuss what the cold does to trees, other than make them cold. Ways to protect them in marginal areas. Some of these things to do will be fun; some of them easy and all will be very useful to help you in protecting them.

Chapter 9 is all about other things that want to eat your precious tree and fruit, other than you. From aphids to white fly and from birds to bird poop like creatures; we will delve into the pests that affect citrus trees and ways to avoid and conquer them.

Chapter 10 will find out what makes your tree sick. We will not cover all of the diseases that bother your trees, that would be a book in of it self. We will talk about the main ones, the ones that you might have a better chance of seeing, hopefully not, but it is best to know about them. The ways to protect your trees from the diseases and ways to rid your self of them, should they happen to appear.

Chapter 11, there are other problems that may come up that don't really fit pests or diseases, they just kind of happen. Some are naturally occurring some can be prevented; still others just take time to fix themselves.

Chapter 12 can be summed up in one word…reproduce. We will discuss the different ways that citrus trees can be propagated, from grafting and rooting, to seed planting. Each has its merits and disadvantages. There are also varying levels of expertise used here, I will break it down to the most elementary methods possible.

Chapter 13, I will wrap this all up in a nice neat little package. I will give you the benefits of all of this, things to share with other people, and how to really have fun with your new hobby.

Chapter 14. What would a book about growing such tasty things be without at least a few of my tips on how to use your fruit?

After reading this introduction, I hope I have you excited about what is inside? The world of growing citrus for your self is a combination of many things, hard work, excitement, perseverance, and with a little luck, success! In the end it will all be worthwhile when you bite into your first, home grown tangerine!

Let's get started!

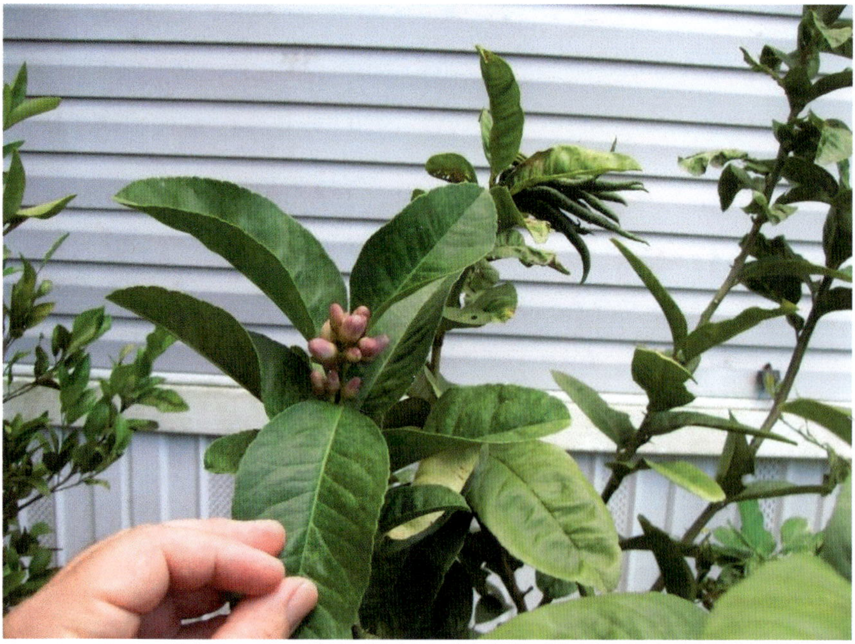

How To Grow Citrus Practically Anywhere

Employees at the Florence Citrus Growers Association packing boxes: Winter Haven, Florida (1934)

CHAPTER 2: The History of Citrus

I will not go into great depth on the history of citrus. There are many fine books out there, both in and out of print. One of the best books, if you can find it, is "The Citrus Industry, Volume 1". It was published in 1967 by the University of California, but sadly is out of print.

It is mostly agreed that citrus are native to the Southeast Asia region. However, the real problem arises when we discuss its movement to the Mediterranean and Americas.

Chinese writings dating back many thousands of years, before the birth of Christ, have descriptions of citrus or citrus type fruit in them. The earliest being in the book "Yu Kung", or Tribute of Yu. This was written about the Emperor Ta Yu, who reigned from 2205 to 2197 B.C. In this book it states "The baskets were filled with woven ornamented silks. The bundle contained small oranges and pummeloes."

Citron is probably the most talked about of the early citrus varieties.

It is unclear how it moved from its native habitat, which has been said is probably India, and spread to so many different places, that many other cultures thought it was indigenous to their locale.

Around 350 BC, Alexander the Great is believed to have been responsible for it being introduced to Europe. Citron today is grown mainly as a novelty, though; the Etrog Citron is still an important part of the Jewish Feast of Tabernacle.

As for the Americas and their place in the history lesson, we can thank Christopher Columbus. He carried citrus over to the New World on his second voyage in 1493. In that year he brought sweet and sour oranges, lemons, limes and citrons to the island of Haiti.

It was not long before they made their way to Mexico. By 1565, Florida was such a wonderful growing environment that sour oranges had become naturalized.

Citrus was becoming an important staple on sailing ships for traveling to the New World. Its vitamin C content was key in helping seaman avoid contracting scurvy and many other diseases.

As years went by, the Spanish missionaries were moving citrus to Arizona in the early 1700's. By the mid 1700's it was in California.

By the mid 1800's a commercial crop of citrus was planted in southern California.

What is now downtown Los Angeles was the site of the state's first commercial farm.

It was well known that Citrus was useful in combating scurvy, so in 1849, when the gold rush hit, citrus was in high demand.

In the early 20th century, Oranges and satsumas, many from trees imported from Japan, were produced along the Texas coast in fairly large quantities as early as 1910, when 42,384 orange trees produced 10,694 boxes of oranges.

Today citrus is grown in many countries and is ever increasing in its range, due mostly to the work of hybridizers.

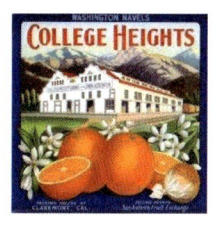

College Heights Washington Navels (Oranges) 1930

COLLEGE HEIGHTS ORANGE & LEMON ASSOCIATION

How To Grow Citrus Practically Anywhere

"Taste is a mystery."
— Daniel Mendelsohn

CHAPTER 3: Cultivars and Taste

    When it comes to citrus and what they taste like, you need to remember, taste is a mystery and extremely relative. There is the old axiom, "There is no accounting for taste".

    I like the taste of sour gummy worms you may not. Does that mean that a certain cultivar of citrus that I enjoy is bad? Of course not! Calalmondins come to mind. My wife can't stand the flavor; I enjoy using them in substitution of anything that has lemon in it. Calamondin meringue pie is one of my favorites. I hear the merits of Meyer Lemons all the time; I am not really fond of them.

So, with all of that being said, I want to list some of the more common citrus that you may be able to find. I will also add some to the list that, with a little digging, you might be able to locate.

This list will have some that, while the flavor is either not worth a plugged nickel, or is useless eating, it is still something fun to grow. I will also try to add some of the reasons why it may or may not be worth your time to grow, i.e. seediness, ability to be peeled easily or it might just be a dog in my eyes.

This list will also be FAR from complete. There are new cultivars being created all the time, some naturally, some man made. Some of these will be basically just rootstock, they are edible, some will even taste like you are being poisoned, I promise, you are not.

Let's start with what I consider the most popular citrus fruit.

Lemon.

Botanically, it is known as Citrus limon.

According to the book, "Citrus Varieties of the World, second edition, published in 2000, lemon production stands just shy of 6 million tons. The United States leads production with a little over 800,000 tons. Do you see why I consider this the most popular fruit? That is a lot of lemonade stands!

Let's start with one of the most famous lemons, the Eureka. This is the lemon that you are probably most familiar with, if you purchase them at the grocery store. It is considered the world's most widely grown lemon.

This plant has sparse foliage and is probably one of the least cold resistant varieties of citrus. The Lisbon lemon, which is also widely grown, is a little more cold resistant. With a vigorous, open growth habit, this one will need to be pruned on occasion to keep it under control in a container. There will be more on pruning later in this book.

It has a medium to thin rind and has a very high juice content, with an equally as high acid level. This fruit is very often seedless, usually no more than 3-4 seeds per fruit if you do find some. This tree, if given the right climate can have a tendency to produce fruit year round.

Flowers are born at the tips of the branches and will have a purple tint to them.

There is also a variegated version of the Eureka. The leaves and fruit will be striped white; the fruit will turn yellow when ripe. The inside flesh is pink.

The Meyer Lemon has the citrus world a buzz, even though it is not a true lemon. It is a cross between a lemon and probably a sweet orange.

This tree was introduced to the United States in 1908 from China. A plant explorer named Frank Meyer found it and brought it here. It has many characteristics of a lemon, the tinted flower, lemon scented foliage and bronze colored new growth. The fruit is what gives away some of its ancestry. It turns yellow like a normal lemon, but will continue changing color to almost orange. The flesh has a nice lemon flavor, but it is sweeter than a normal lemon, probably from its orange parent. Meyer lemons have been reported to handle temperatures down to 20 degrees before dying.

There is one more lemon I would like to discuss, the ponderosa lemon. This is most definitely a lemon-citron hybrid. The juice content is much lower than the Eureka or Lisbon, but what it lacks in percentage of juice, it makes up in size, in two ways. The tree itself will only grow to about half the size of a true lemon. The fruit will be much larger, sometimes over two pounds. It has bumpy rind, is impossible to peel and has a great many seeds, but what a conversation piece!

There are many more wonderful varieties out there, just to name a few: Bearss, Genova, and Harvey. I encourage you to look for some of these, as you will not be disappointed.

The Lime

There are actually two different types of limes, one being more acidic, seedy and small. This is the Citrus aurantifolia type. This list consists of the Key Lime or also known as the Mexican Lime.

The other, being larger and seedless is Citrus latifolia. This list consists of the Persian or Tahiti Lime. The funny part about the name of this lime is, this variety is neither grown in Tahiti nor Persia, which is now actually Iran.

The history of this lime is extremely obscure; it probably came from the Orient through Persia, then onto Brazil and Australia. Records indicate that it was grown in the later as early as 1824. Then it came through Tahiti and finally showed up in California in the second half of the 19th century. If this is not confusing enough, the Persian lime is called Bearrs lime in California. So if you see, Persian, Tahiti or Bearrs lime, it is different names for the same fruit.

Persian limes do not contain any viable pollen, so they will almost always be seedless. They are very juicy and extremely acidic.

The other lime I mentioned, Citrus aurantifolia, is often called a true lime as well as West Indian, Mexican or Key lime. At one time this particular lime was grown in the Florida Keys; it only has a small presence there now.

This tree is fairly vigorous; medium sized, and has a bushy growth habit. It also has many thorns. The largest downfall to this particular tree is its extreme sensitivity to cold. It is much more prone to damage then its cousin, the Persian lime. Another oddity to this lime, when allowed to ripen on the tree, it is a yellow-green color or actually a full yellow, such as a lemon. It is usually harvested when still dark green.

Another lime that you may stumble across is the Kieffer lime. Citrus hystrix as it is known botanically. Very frost tender, has little juice, and is extremely aromatic. The claim to fame for this lime is the leaves of the tree. They are used in Southeast Asia to flavor curries and soups. It also goes by the name Makrut or Indonesian lime.

One last lime that I will mention, that you may run across, is not even a lime! The Rangpur lime, Citrus limonia, is a common rootstock and is actually an acidic mandarin. It is only referred to as a lime because of the acidity; it does not even taste like a lime.

Mainly grown for rootstock or as an ornamental, it is relatively cold hardy and in a pinch, can be substituted for lemons or limes. Very seedy and is a rather pretty reddish orange.

Oranges

Oranges are probably one of the first things that you think of when discussing citrus type fruits. They are sweet, readily available, and have a wide array of uses.

They can be broken down into four, separate groups:

Navel oranges, Common oranges, Pigmented oranges and Sugar or Acidless oranges.

Navel oranges have just that, a navel or belly button. The area where the navel is is also called the apex. This apex is where a rudimentary secondary fruit is located.

Navel oranges are the earliest ripening of all of the oranges. They are usually seedless and larger than most. Being sweet and fairly easy to peel are among there biggest draws.

There are a few downfalls to this group. The tree itself is less vigorous a grower and less productive, which, in container growing, could actually be classified as a good thing.

They also tend to not be as able to adapt to certain climates. They prefer the Mediterranean type of climates and are not suited to many regions where other oranges perform well. Navel oranges also tend to have less fruit than most of their counterparts.

Some noteworthy navel oranges that you might come across would include the Washington navel. This particular variety is the time honored standard. It was introduced to California from Brazil in 1873. For many it is unmatched in flavor and ease of peeling. It has a drooping growth habit and the fruit matures early. It does not do well however if there is a lot of hot dry weather during flowering.

Cara Cara red navel orange originated a sport of Washington and was discovered in Venezuela in 1976. It was introduced to the USA in 1977 and released in 1987.

For the most part it shows all the same characteristics as the Washington, fruit size as well as most of the other features. The navel tends to be a bit smaller and of course the pigmentation is colored. The rind usually does not show any blush color except on occasion, depending on the season. The flavor is good but lacks the distinct flavor of a true blood orange. This variety could very possibly live up to its name, in Italian, Cara means beloved. There are a number of other navel oranges out there, but chances are, these two will be the easiest to find.

Common oranges, at one time in their history, where referred to as blond oranges. No, they were not beach bums with sun-drenched hair. They were called that to distinguish them from the pigmented oranges and navels. Common oranges are probably the largest group of citrus, other than mandarins, in regards to tree growth and fruit characteristics.

Commercially, common oranges are further divided into seediness and flavor categories. Seeds are not an important factor when it comes to juicing operations as opposed to flavor and sugar content. In the fresh fruit market, seeds can be a real hindrance to the popularity of a variety.

As I mentioned earlier, this group is very large and you might come across an endless array of them. I will discuss a few that I have tried and enjoyed.

Ambersweet, released in 1989 is actually a hybrid, resulting from another hybrid. The mix of this particular fruit is one half sweet orange, one-quarter grapefruit and one-quarter mandarin. A true mutt! Though, it is classified as an orange. The tree itself is vigorous and upright growing. It has a moderate cold hardiness; it was actually bred for this very reason. It can easily handle down to the mid-to-low twenties. It actually is better suited for a cooler, less humid area; such as it is in central Florida.

Hamlin orange actually came to be as a chance seedling, discovered in 1879. It has relatively small fruit, only averaging about 3-4 inches in diameter, which is sometimes too small for the fresh fruit market. It has a very high juice content and is one of the earliest to ripen, so the juice industry loves them. The fruit is not difficult to peel, but does have a tendency to split on the tree from time to time. Usually seedless, the occasional seed will arise. It is probably one of the easiest to find in your local big box store or garden center.

The Parson Brown orange originated in 1856 as a seedling at the home of Reverend N.L. Brown near Webster, Florida. In 1874 it was propagated and the variety was named Parson Brown. It has high juice content, very productive and a vigorous grower. Sweet and well flavored is among its many attributes, however, it tends to be very seedy with an average of 15 seeds per fruit.

The Pineapple orange is of interest to me because of its origin. It was thought to have been brought to Charleston, SC from China, and planted by another Reverend.

J.B. Owens planted it in 1860 at Sparr, Florida. How it got its unusual name is somewhat of a debated topic. Some people say the tree was shaped like a pineapple while others maintain that it resembled a pineapple in either smell or flavor. It is a very productive tree, however, one of the downsides to this variety is its tendency to alternate bear.

Basically, you will have an excellent crop one year and a much lighter crop the next. This can be alleviated to some degree by thinning the fruit on heavy years. With a high juice content, good color and very sweet, rich flavor, I highly recommend this one.

Kumquats
Kumquats originated in China (they are noted in literature dating to the 12th century), and have long been cultivated there and in Japan. They were introduced to Europe in 1846 by Robert Fortune, collector for the London Horticultural Society, and shortly thereafter into North America. Originally placed in the genus Citrus, they were transferred to the genus Fortunella in 1915.

Kumquats are frequently eaten raw. As the rind is sweet and the juicy center is sour, the raw fruit is usually consumed either whole or only the rind is eaten. The fruit is considered ripe when it reaches a yellowish-orange stage, and has just shed the last tint of green.

There are 4 or 5 different species of kumquats, but you probably only be able to really find three of them, unless you are really hardcore and search high and low.

Fortunella crassifolia - Meiwa Kumquat. This is the round kumquat, often confused with the calamondin, which is a kumquat hybrid. Meiwa is considered the sweeter of the two most common kumquats.

Fortunella japonica - Marumi or Nagami Kumquat is the other of the most common. This is the oval kumquat that you will often find in gift baskets around Christmas time.

The final, more common kumquat is the Fortunella hindsii - Hong Kong Kumquat. This is the smallest-fruited of the kumquats with round fruits that rarely exceed one-half inch in diameter. The tree is very small and very spiny and the leaves are small and narrow. The fruits are red-orange at maturity and hold on the tree well. The rind is thin, and there are several large seeds in each fruit; thus, the fruit is virtually inedible. Although small, the Chinese are said to prize these fruits and they preserve them in honey for use as a spicy flavoring.

Tangerines

In my opinion, tangerines are the most popular of the dooryard citrus to grow. Just as a side note, if you see the words, tangerine, satsuma or mandarin, they are basically three words for the same fruit. Think tangerine.

The tangerine is an orange-colored citrus fruit that is closely related to, or possibly a type of, mandarin orange. In terms of taste, both oranges and tangerines are sweet, with the tangerines being less tart. They are also much easier to peel.

When it comes to varieties, the mandarins have everybody beat! I am only going to list a few, there are so many good ones, and an entire book can be written on these alone. I will start off with my wife's favorite one.

Seedless Kishu produces very sweet, seedless, and easy to peel fruit. Since the fruit is small and soft, it is not grown commercially, but does great for the regular homegrown farmer.

Dancy Tangerine has a rich, spicy flavor. Dark orange-red, with a smooth, thin rind. Peels easily. Flesh is a deep orange. It is smaller than the other mandarins, and very seedy. This is the traditional Christmas "tangerine."

Ponkan or Chinese Honey Mandarin is of ancient origins in India or China. They are very sweet and aromatic, somewhat dry. The flesh and rind are deep orange, with very few seeds.

Clementine or Algerian Tangerine is a juicy, sweet, mild to rich flavor, with excellent taste. They are a Medium-small to medium sized and usually seedless flesh. The rind is deep orange to orange-red, smooth and glossy. Can be peeled very easily. They ripen in late fall into winter: Originated and grown in North Africa they are now grown extensively in California since 1914.

The tangerine or mandarin class has many, many hybrids associated with it. Here are a few of the more notable ones.

Tangelo is a hybrid between a mandarin and a grapefruit. There are two notable varieties: 'Minneola' which is a bright orange-red and has the distinctive neck, you have seen these in the store. It has a rich, tart tangerine flavor when picked late and some seeds. 'Orlando' has small fruit with a mild, sweet flavor and is seedy. A third tangelo, 'Sampson' has a grapefruit like flavor.

Fairchild is cross between 'Clementine' mandarin and a 'Orlando' tangelo. It is rich flavored, juicy and sweet, especially when very ripe. It has an Orange flesh, medium to medium-small and round. The red-orange rind is somewhat difficult to peel.

There are of course, many more. I encourage you to seek as many out as you can and try the fruit before committing to a certain one. You can also grow numerous ones and judge them for yourself.

Grapefruit

I will not go into great detail about grapefruit, only for the simple fact of, they can get really big, and unless you are super serious about this, not recommended for container culture. It can be done, I am, but there are times I am struggling with the trees in the winter.

The grapefruit was known as the shaddock or shattuck until the 19th century. Its current name alludes to clusters of the fruit on the tree, which often appear similar to how grapes grow. Botanically, it was not distinguished from the pomelo (which is what was one of the crosses to create a grapefruit) until the 1830s, when it was given the name Citrus paradisi.

There are many varieties of grapefruit, which include, the Oro Blanco (white flesh), Ruby Red (red flesh), Thompson (pink flesh), White Marsh (white flesh), Flame (red flesh), Star Ruby (red flesh), Duncan (white flesh). If you can get a grapefruit that is grafted onto a dwarfing rootstock, you will be okay. Planted from seed, it will take 10-12 years to grow fruit and it will be a very large tree.

In closing this chapter, you have probably surmised that there are a huge number of varieties and cultivars of citrus. The only limits are, what you like to eat and room to grow them! Here is one last little list of a few other things to search out, I wish I could post everything there is out there, but I am not sure I would still be alive by the time I got them all listed.

Calamondin- A kumquat hybrid.

Ujukitsu Lemon- It ripens to a bright yellow with an interesting pear-shaped form that's quite large, often bigger than a softball. Thought to be a strain of Tangelo, a cross between a grapefruit and a tangerine, the fruit is amazingly sweet and juicy with a thick rind that peels easily.

Eustis Limequat- Often jokingly called a "useless limequat' this one is a cross between a lime and a kumquat, with mostly a lime like taste.

Yuzu- became popular in the U.S. culinary scene in the early 2000's and it can still be found today on restaurant menus in the form of sauces, cocktails and desserts. The fresh fruit is difficult to find in the U.S. but you can purchase yuzu in various forms including bottled juice, dry powder and in a paste form.

Trifoliate Orange (Flying Dragon) is an ornamental citrus, with nice smelling flowers. The fruit is about golf ball size, slightly fuzzy, and extremely seedy. As for the plant and fruits uses, it is good for rootstock, hybridization and target practice! The fruit is edible, you will think you are being poisoned, but you will be fine. The taste is wonderful, if you enjoy the taste of kerosene.

Poncirus trifoliate in flower with a new flush of leaves.

How To Grow Citrus Practically Anywhere

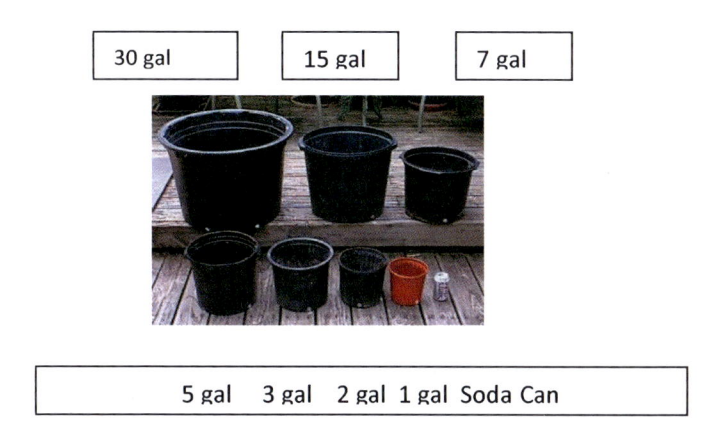

| 30 gal | 15 gal | 7 gal |

| 5 gal   3 gal   2 gal 1 gal Soda Can |

Common Pot Sizes

Chapter 4 Your Citrus Trees House

There are all kinds of materials that can be used to house your citrus tree.

Everything from ornamental, fancy type containers made of ceramic to the common nursery type black pot (see above) and numerous things in between. I have seen people using plastic pickle buckets, Rubbermaid containers and even garbage cans.

The basic concept should always be the same, holes for drainage, ability to stand up to the elements, and a large enough capacity to hold the needed soil.

The first item I mentioned, holes for drainage. This is kind of a no brainer if you ask me. There are very few plants that can survive in a water-laden environment and citrus is certainly not one of them. They enjoy a moist soil (see chapter 7 on light and water) but they do not like wet feet. In other words, they can't live in a swamp. Holes provide the drainage for the extra water to come out. The holes themselves do not need to be very large, matter of fact; too large can be a bad thing too. If they are too large, the soil will come out every time you water. If the container you choose does have extremely large holes, a small piece of chicken wire fence over it will rectify that. I have seen people use shattered clay pot pieces or rocks, those will work, but it will take up a lot of room and it just adds weight to the container. If you just said to yourself, the added weight won't allow the tree to topple over in the wind, then your tree is in too small a container. Go up a size or two.

The second item I mentioned, ability to stand up to the elements. Face it; cardboard would not make for a good container to grow your plant in. It would be okay to take it traveling to a friend as a gift, but not for any extended time.

I have a friend that uses those large carry all containers, the ones that have rope handles. They are fine for a year, maybe two if you are very lucky, but they are not designed to withstand the ultra violet rays of the sun. They dry out, crack, and eventually just fall apart. Plastic pots are made of special plastic that is designed for outdoor use.

The next question usually asked is, what size pot should I use? Well, that will, of course, depend on the size of the tree. A small tree that is only a foot or two tall will only need a three-gallon pot. I work in the nursery trade, so the sizes I mention will be "trade" gallons. You can see a picture of the different sizes above. The soda can is for reference.

If you are somebody that relies more on actual numbers, these are approximate:

Width x Height
30 gallon = 26" x 18"
15 gallon = 18" x 16"
7 gallon = 14" x 12"
5 gallon = 12" x 11"
3 gallon = 10" x 9"
2 gallon = 8" x 8"
1 gallon = 7" x 6"

As the tree gets bigger, you naturally will want to go to a bigger pot. How big should you go? However big you can handle. I deal with nurseries that handle 65 and 100-gallon pots, these things are huge. You would need a front-end loader to move them or at least 5 or 6 strong guys. I don't recommend these. Once a tree gets to a decent size, I try to keep them in nothing bigger than a 30 gallon.

You can keep them in a 15 gallon for a few years, but once they start to slow down in production or lose their vigor, it is time to move up or do some root pruning.

Root pruning is a very simple procedure, to discuss. However, when the rubber meets the road, it can be a tad messy and cumbersome. The basic idea is to remove the tree from the pot it is in and cut off a bunch of roots. I usually recommend about one third. The key here is, however much of the roots you cut off, remember to cut off the same amount of the canopy. If you cut more canopy off than roots that is okay, you will just set the tree back a little more. If you cut off more roots than canopy, then the tree can not support itself and could very easily die.

After you do all of this cutting, repot the tree in fresh soil back into the same container. You should be good to go for at least 2 years. Don't be alarmed if you don't get as many fruit, you cut a bunch of it off, but the tree will be fine.

I am asked many times, which is better, plastic or clay/terracotta? Each has their advantages and disadvantages. Personally, I prefer plastic. They are lighter and easier to pick up and move. They are much cheaper and easier to find. They also don't tend to allow the soil to dry out as quickly, and in the middle of the summer, you will be thankful for that!

Terracotta pots tend to be earthy colors, so they look prettier. They also stay cooler than the black nursery pots. I had a friend of mine do an experiment once. He took a black, nursery trade pot and put it in full sunshine, you know, the type of light the citrus tree needs, and then stuck a soil thermometer in it. The temperature rose to 120 degrees!! Imagine your feet staying in that kind of heat all day, you would not be happy. This is where terracotta pots come in handy. You can also use a colored pot OR get some of that plastic spray paint used for outdoor furniture and paint the pot white or terracotta, if you so desire. That color will reflect much of the suns rays and keep the pot a tad cooler.

So the tree itself does not really care what kind of pot you use, this is your decision. You just have to keep in mind, functionality, cost, and what, if at all, you really care what it looks like.

The last thing pertaining to pots that I will leave you with is this. Make sure you keep an eye out on the roots coming from the bottom of the container, they can be very advantageous.

How To Grow Citrus Practically Anywhere

"It is impossible to have a healthy and sound plant, without a proper respect for the soil."
Darren Sheriff

Chapter 5 The Dirt on Potting Soil

This is another one of those topics that, if you ask five different people, what type of soil they prefer, you might get six answers!

There are those that like coconut husks and sand. Some like the peat and pine bark mix. Others use sand, perlite, peat and pine. Personally, I like whatever I can find.

No, this is not a cop out. I have many trees growing in different types of medium; I see very little difference in growth. Working at a nursery, I have access to all of the soil I want, within reason of course. We use fine pine bark and some sand.

Some of my other mixtures have been these two things, some peat, perlite, vermiculite and compost. If you do not want to play around with mixing your own potting mix, there are already made concoctions out there. There are even companies that sell a Citrus/Cactus mix that works very well.

If you haven't caught on yet, there is really no "specific" soil mix you should use.

There ARE however some basics that you need to keep in mind.

Good drainage is the number one item. I have mentioned before and will mention again, citrus need lots of moisture, but they don't like wet feet. The soil needs to be very well draining, yet, will retain some moisture. Sand is great at draining, but has little, to no, water retention. Peat moss holds water extremely well, but does not drain too well. A combination of these two with some perlite, which acts as drainage. is acceptable. I mentioned coco husks earlier. This is something relatively new to the market, at least new to me. The claim to fame is, it holds water like peat moss, is more earth friendly and does not break down as fast as peat.

The one thing you never want to use is soil directly from your garden. It usually contains too much clay, even in the best of areas, and in a compact area, with the amount of heat that is put upon the container; you will end up with a giant brick. There is also the chance of contamination, nematodes and/or other unwanted organisms introduced with straight garden soil.

Here are some tips to think about when you are choosing your ingredients.

They need to be able to be rewetted. Some peat and bark media are very difficult to re-wet if they are allowed to dry out. If you keep a consistent moisture level (See Chapter 7) this may only be a minor problem. Along these same lines, you do not want something that will shrink away from the side of the pot as it dries.

You will want to create the optimum weight for the size plant and pot. You do not want to use something that is very heavy, as sand comes to mind. Nor do not want to use something that is so light that your plants blow over. You will need to find the balance between these.

The measurement of pH is something else to consider. Citrus prefer the range of 5.5 to 6.5, slightly acidic. Peat moss for instance is around 4.0 (Very Acidic). Sand is neutral in its pH at 7.0 as well as perlite. The reason coconut coir is often used; it is already in the 5.5-6.5 ranges. Pine bark is acidic, but not as much as the Peat Moss. Well aged manures, composts, and assorted other amendments are all used in combinations to change your pH. Adding ground calcitic limestone or agricultural lime raises the pH and contains calcium, which strengthens cell walls. Dolomitic limestone, sometimes used instead of calcitic limestone, also raises the pH; and this supplies magnesium as well as calcium. Make sure you follow the directions according to the package. These all come in different strengths and from different manufacturers. If you are unsure of what the pH is of the mix you created, get it tested at your local extension office. It is usually a very nominal charge.

You have probably heard that a good mix will be light and fluffy. When it is done correctly, you are allowing air pockets to form in the soil structure so your plant roots and microorganisms have the oxygen they need to survive.

So there you have it, the dirt on soil for your citrus. As long as you have the basics in place, your tree will be very happy and healthy in its home. Isn't this your goal?

How To Grow Citrus Practically Anywhere

Healthy Looking, well fed Kumquats

CHAPTER 6: Orange you going to Feed Me?

    Fertilizers and feeding your citrus trees can be a very diverse subject. If you ask 5 people what they like to use, you will get 6 answers! Seems like you have heard that before!

    Like most of this book, I will tell you what I have found works for me, sprinkled with as much scientific information as I know.

    Let's start with some of the scientific stuff.

    I mentioned in the previous chapter about citrus needing a pH of 5.5-6.5. Have you ever really wondered why a certain pH is good for a plant?

    PH is not an indication of fertility, but it does affect the availability of fertilizer nutrients. The soil may contain adequate nutrients yet an unfavorable pH level may limit plant health. Simply speaking, if the pH is out of whack, you can have all the nutrients in the world in your soil, but if the plant can't use them, you will see signs of deficiency. Of all the major fertilizer nutrients, nitrogen is the main nutrient affecting soil pH, and soils can become more acidic or more alkaline depending on the type of nitrogen fertilizer used. The Nitrate-based products are the least acidifying of the nitrogen fertilizers, while ammonium-based products have the greatest potential to acidify soil. The fertilizer package will tell you what it is made from.

With all of that being said, citrus trees are heavy nitrogen feeders. Nitrogen is the first number of the three on a fertilizer bag, such as 5-2-6. The five being the nitrogen, in this example. This is actually the preferred ratio that citrus like. I will let you in on a dirty little secret here, while this is their preferred ratio, it is not set in concrete. If you have something, say with slightly different ratios, or a 10-10-10, that will work just fine.

Personally, I have found a product that I fell in love with as soon as I started using it. I do not work for this company, nor do I have any affiliation with them, I just like their stuff. It is called Citrus-Tone. The company that manufactures it is Espoma. They also make things such as Holly-Tone, Tomato-Tone, etc. After I started using it, I saw very good results almost immediately. That is not to say that it is the end all or be all in fertilizers. I have had discussions with people that hate the stuff and use things that I do not like. Remember I said, you would get all kinds of answers if you ask enough people?

There are fertilizers on the market that I just don't like. I will not name names, some of them remind me of fish gravel, and others are stake like. Speaking of which, please do not use the plant stakes. Again, this is my personnel opinion, sprinkled with some knowledge.

Nitrogen moves through the soil very easily, matter of fact, every time you water a plant; you are leaching nitrogen out. The second number, phosphorous, and the third number, potassium do not move as easily.

Okay, the scene is set. If you use these stakes, the nitrogen will move out to the plant roots like it is suppose to, great! The phosphorous and potassium do not, they just sit there. The roots go through the soil on their happy little way when they encounter this blob of fertilizer. ZAP! They get burned because it is such an intense concentration of fertilizer. Not good. Those stakes also contain a good amount of salts, which, to me, does not sound like a good idea either.

So, let's say you cannot find Citrus-Tone in your local store and you are leery of purchasing things online, no problem. I mentioned earlier that you could use other things. Holly-Tone will make a good substitution. Citrus trees are also on the acidic side in their pH needs, so the Holly-Tone will work just fine.

How often you feed them will also be a matter of debate. Using one of the products above, what I have found works is, every 6 weeks, throw a couple of tablespoons on the top of the soil and water it in. If you are planning on protecting the trees during the winter cold months, you can feed them all year. If you can leave them outside and it will be getting cold, see the "protect me" chapter 8 in this book. Start feeding them about Valentines Day and stop feeding them about Labor Day. Are these dates steadfast? No, a week or two before and after each of them is fine; they are just easier to remember. The theory is, you want to allow the new growth to harden off before winter sets in at the tail end of the season. You also do not want the plant to flush new growth too early at the beginning of the season. Also, when it comes to the earlier feeding time, most fertilizers need to be broken down by the soil microbes before the plant can use them. Feeding in February will give those microbes some time and the nutrients will be ready when the plant wakes up and needs them.

If you want to give your trees a special treat, hey, they can be just like children; mine are, you can give them a foliar feeding of fish emulsion every so often. There really is no set time to do this, or how often, though you want to stay within the time frame I mentioned for non-protected plants. If you plan on bringing them inside, you will probably want to stop using it a little earlier, this stuff can really stink, and you don't want that smell in your house. You may also entice your feline friends, if you have any, to want to chomp on the tree if it smells a little fishy.

Liquid fertilizer is a nice treat too! I try to think of it more as a candy for my trees. Citrus-Tone is organic, and tends to feed the soil, where liquid feeds the tree. It can also be used in the same manner as the fish emulsion, just without as much smell.

Another thing about different fertilizers, and again, I am sure there are different opinions on this. Slow release fertilizers. I use them, on occasion. It is more of a backup plan than a full-blown fertilizer regiment. Remember, I said that citrus are heavy nitrogen feeders? In my humble opinion, slow release is just that, slow. If they need a higher amount of N, then the slow release will not be able to supply it. Think of it as a slow trickle of food, it is there in the background, but not the real meal.

You have also probably heard the old adage, "Even too much of a good thing is bad"?

This can go for fertilizing your citrus trees. Fertilizer burn is a common problem. It's when the very tips of the plant start to die, or when the edges around the leaves look as if they have been "burned." The most common culprit in this situation is salt. Salts are used in fertilizers; remember I mentioned that with the stakes? So if you're fertilizing too frequently or applying too much at once, salt will build up in the potting soil and show up as the burned leaves. You will often see white deposits on the soil if you have a heavy hand with the fertilizer. To remedy the situation, flush the salts out of your potting soil by watering the pot deeply until water flows quickly out of the pot. Make sure that the soil has not pulled away from the sides or become "hydrophobic" or you will be getting a false sense of flushing these salts out if the water runs right out. Something to think about here, if you have a home water softening system, many of them use salt. Be careful if you use well water, sometimes salt will leach into it and cause issues also.

Your remedies for this is actually quite easy, install a rain barrel and use that, or purchase cheap bottled water. I will discuss water more in Chapter 7. In the meantime, remember to feed your plants, so they will be able to feed you!

How To Grow Citrus Practically Anywhere

Is there anything more loyal than the sun? ~Mary Oliver

CHAPTER 7: Light and Water

    Light and water, for some reason, seem to be two things that baffle many people when it comes to growing citrus. I want to start with the sun or light requirements. These plants need, what is called, full sun.

    Citrus need 8 or more hours a day of sun. Bare minimum would be 6. Though, with that few of hours your fruit production will be much lower than is possible, if at all, for that plant. Your tree will also not be able to make as much food for itself at that light level. Is it possible to have fruit? Yes. It will be just sparse or sporadic.

I mentioned "full sun". I was working an event one time, answering questions pertaining to gardening and horticulture in general. The fact came up that I knew a lot about citrus. This gentleman approached me with a problem. He said he had this lemon tree that just won't produce any flowers or fruit. I asked him if it was getting full sun, he said yes. I then proceeded to go through my checklist of other possible problems, such as water, fertilizer, soil, container vs. in-ground, etc. Everything seemed to be fine. I then went back to the sunlight issue. I asked him again, are you sure it is getting full sun? He again said, yes. Puzzled, and getting frustrated, I went one more time to the light issue, from a different angle. If you had to give me an amount of hours that the tree received, how many would you say? What he said next was like the heavens opened up and there where a choir of angels singing. What was his answer? FOUR

I was relieved that we finally came up with the answer to his dilemma. It was an easy fix after that, get it more sun.

What is the moral of this story? Just because you walk out into the yard and the sun is shining on your tree, does not mean it is getting full sun. You need to take into account the amount of sun it is receiving all day. With that being said, as I mentioned in Chapter 4, too much sun can also be an issue with the roots.

Watering your tree is a little more complicated. Citrus love moisture, yet do not like to sit in water all the time. This is why you need a well draining soil mix that will also retain some water; see Chapter 5 "The Dirt on Potting Soil".

How much water is enough? Well, as I explained in Chapter 5, this will depend largely on the type of soil you use. There is a sentence in many gardening books that drives me insane. It states, "You should give this plant (whatever it may be) at least one inch of water per week". Let me explain why this is a stupid sentence. If you use a sand based soil mixture or one that is very free draining, how long do you think that one inch of water will last? 30 minutes, maybe? Especially, if it is a bright and sunny, warm day. Now, if you happen to use a more peat based soil or some other mixture that has a lot of water holding capacity to it, how long will that last? A month? 6 weeks? This will also depend on the weather, cool, cloudy will not allow as much transpiration.

How much water is enough, or too much?!

What is the answer to this dilemma? I am glad you asked.

There are two methods that I use, sometimes in combination of each other.

The first one is, I give the plant the finger. I use my index finger, stick it in the soil, if it is dry to the second knuckle, I water the plant. If it still feels damp, I wait a couple of days, and then test it again.

The second method I use on a more regular basis. This one involves a little more work. I like this method because it will also let you know if the soil has pulled away from the sides or has become "hydrophobic", remember me mentioning that last chapter?

First, water the plant until you are absolutely sure it is at maximum capacity. Then, either lift the pot or tip it to one side. Whichever way you do this, it is to get the feel of the weight of the pot. After a couple of days, when you think the tree needs some water, lift or tilt again. Does it still feel pretty heavy? Then you should wait a few more days.

After that time has expired, do the lift/tip again. Do this until it feels approximately half as heavy as it did the first time. I use this method and it works for me. I usually end up watering about every other to every third day in the summer.

This method works well if you have numerous size pots next to each other. As you can imagine, a very small pot will need water long before a large pot.

This is also where the well draining potting soil woks out well. If you do tend to over water plants, as long as the drainage is working, it is actually very hard to give your citrus tree too much water.

The next part is strictly an observation that I have noticed with my citrus trees. I will be up front and say, there is NO scientific evidence of this that I can find, so take it for what it might be worth.

If I have a citrus tree that is not being watered enough, the leaves tend to curl up. You can see in the picture below. I purposely did not water this tree for a week, just to see how long it would take to start rolling the leaves. My plants hate me at times. It survived, and no plants were harmed in the making of this picture.

If a citrus tree is being over-watered, the leaves will get droopy and hang down. Again, I have no scientific proof of this, but I have seen it happen. I really don't want to push a tree the other way myself, and over water it, it is too hard to bring back from that state of decline.

However, I did find this picture of a Kaffir Lime, I would like to credit the photographer, but can't find the name. He was smart in repotting it the tree might be saved.

So, as you can see, sunlight and water play a very important role in your fruit production. Moderation, as in all things, is the key.

How To Grow Citrus Practically Anywhere

Republic of Texas Orange, after a night of 18 degrees, North Charleston, SC

CHAPTER 8: Protect Me

    Cold weather is probably, no, THE main reason not everybody can grow citrus. That goes without saying really. Other than sun and amount of usable space, what other reason could there be? The cold is probably the main reason you bought this book. As I had mentioned earlier in the book, heat can also be a problem, but easier to remedy.

Just as a side note, if you are going to be trying to grow citrus in the ground, you would want to plant it on the south or west side of your house. Those are the two warmest places.

Being that we are talking about growing them in containers, amount of sun is really the only variable that you need to worry about.

In Chapter 4, we discussed the pot that your plant should be in. Chapter 5 dealt with the soil. This chapter will discuss your biggest challenge, winter protection.

Citrus can handle down to 28 degrees for short periods of time. There are, of course, some cultivars that can handle colder. Your lemons and limes are usually the most cold sensitive.

The 28 degrees is dependent on your previous weather conditions. Citrus do not go completely dormant, like your maples and oaks. They go more into a semi-dormancy, which means they never lose their leaves, but do have a dormant type state of no growth.

The previous weather conditions play a major role in the degree of damage that your tree can obtain.

For example, if the weather has been rather chilly, let's say highs in the 40's and dropping down to the low and mid thirties at night. Then you have a night down in the upper twenties, your tree should not obtain very much damage at all. It will sail through, unscathed.

However, if you have been in the mid 60's by day and only in the 50's or 40's at night, then drop to 30 one night, your tree will have a much higher possibility of being damaged. The reason, the tree had a chance to get ready for that cold weather.

This really goes for in ground or in container grown trees. You should also take into account that in a container, it is up in the air, so the soil will get colder faster.

This is where being in a container comes in handy. If really cold weather is coming, you can bring the tree into your unheated garage. As long as it stays right at or above freezing, it will be fine. You can keep it this way for at least a couple of days. If it is possible, bring the tree back out the next day to receive some sunlight and fresh air.

If you live in a climate that that kind of weather will be around for weeks on end, then we need to go to step two.

A sunroom would be the ideal situation, lots of sun, warmth and people for it to talk to. I understand that not everybody has the "ideal" situation. As long as you have some kind of large room, i.e. a spare bedroom, garage, etc, we can still make this work.

You will need to invest in some kind of grow light system. It certainly does not need to be elaborate! There are all kinds of lighting systems out there, you just need to figure out, how much this hobby and the possibility of home grown citrus is worth to you.

I have seen things as simple as a couple of workshop lights pointed directly at the trees, to an elaborate system of chain hung fluorescent lights on timers.

As long as the plants are getting an adequate amount of the different bands of light they require, using indoor lighting is no problem.

Making sure that your plants are well watered before any kind of cold weather is also extremely important. A well-hydrated, healthy plant will be able to handle cold much better than one that is dry and sickly. This is where your fertilizer program is crucial. Make sure that you stick to a constant routine, like it was stated in Chapter 6, in a protected container, your tree can be fed year round.

As I alluded to back in Chapter 4, black pots can also get very hot. I told you about that friend of mine in Colorado doing a test one time.

Can you imagine having your feet in 120 degrees all day?

The problem with a black pot is, it absorbs the suns light. If you have ever stepped onto black asphalt in the middle of summer on a sunny day, you know how hot something black can get.

There are, of course, ways to help alleviate this problem.

One of my favorites is the easiest, use a pot in a pot system. The pot that the tree is in can be of any color; black is usually the most common one. The outside pot will need to be a size or two larger and preferably a light color, such as white. It could even be terracotta, if you want it to be pretty. Between the layer of space between the pots and the light color of the outside pot reflecting the suns rays, it will remain at least a few degrees cooler. Every little bit helps.

You can also eliminate the outside pot and just paint the pot that your plant is in. There are paints on the market that are designed for painting plastics. I prefer white, but any light color will work. Here is another little trick. Only paint one half of the pot with the paint. Leave one half black. Why? During the heat of the summer, turn the white half to the west or hottest side. During the spring and fall, turn it 180 degrees so the dark side is facing the hotter side. It will keep the soil warmer and the tree will continue to grow. If you are lucky enough to have a mild winter I would leave the dark side to the west.

If you don't like either of these ideas, there is a third option; however, it will only be good during the regular growing season, unless again, you have mild winters.

Plant other plants around the container to help shade it. These could be your favorite flowers or maybe some herbs. The key to remember here however is, they will need to have about the same water requirements as your citrus tree. Cactus growing around the pot will most definitely be a bad idea.

While your plant is inside, you will want to probably have a dish of some kind under the tree to catch excess water. Make sure you empty it once the pot has stopped draining.

The humidity in your house can play havoc with a citrus tree too. I can't even begin to count the times that I have had a panic phone call or e-mail, telling me their citrus tree is dropping all of its leaves. Other than maybe putting a humidifier in the room with your tree, or placing it in or near a bathroom that has a shower, there is not much you can do. It will drop its leaves, but it should not die. When it comes back outside in the spring, it will flush all new growth.

Speaking of flushing new growth, did you notice the picture at the start of this chapter? The Republic of Texas Orange that had been left outside in 18 degrees, in North Charleston.

Here is what it looked like the following year!

It did not produce any fruit that year, due to the fact that it had to put so much energy into new leaf production. It did fruit the following year. Very tough tree!

Back in Chapter 6, I had discussed the feeding schedule of Citrus that you will be protecting, versus, one that is in the ground. To demonstrate what can happen if you feed too late and to tie in to this chapter on cold protection, let me show you the result of not following these rules.

I am one that likes to push a plant to see what it can do. So, one winter I decided to construct a cold frame and stuck all of the citrus in it. I continued to feed it as if it were completely protected. Well, it got warm, and the trees started to put out a new flush of growth. Then, a real cold spell set in and the outside temperature dropped to another 18 degrees two nights in a row. I had an electric heater in there, but it just could not keep up. The temperature bottomed out at 30, which would not have been bad, but for the new growth, it was deadly. Take a look.

Notice how all the other leaves around the damage are fine? That was new growth I am holding in my hand, or at least it was. This is a Cocktail Grapefruit. The tree ended up no worse the wear, I cut off the damaged section and you would never have known.

Here is one more. You will notice the other leaves; I had even watered it hoping for some assistance. The new growth was just too tender. Moral: Know approximately how cold it will get so you can follow a fertilizer program and not suffer this problem.

How To Grow Citrus Practically Anywhere

The Giant Swallowtail Butterfly

CHAPTER 9 Pests:

When compared to other fruit trees, citrus are basically carefree. They tolerate an amazing amount of neglect and still fruit reliably. Keeping citrus in optimal health will require some vigilance though as they are prone to a myriad of pests.

Scale, spider mites, aphids, citrus leaf miners, whitefly, as well as others, all attack citrus. If you want to look at the bright side, more times than not, you will not have to fight all of these critters at the same time. One year may be bad with aphids; the next year will be bad with whitefly. Doesn't that make you feel better?

Here is a list of some of the main pests and what can be done about them.

Cottony Cushion Scale

Soft Brown Scale

Black Scale

Mealy Bugs on Navel Orange

    SCALE & MEALY BUGS are white, brown or orange stationary insects that suck plant juices. They are most common on the undersides of leaves. Scale can be controlled with horticultural oil and/or a non-systemic insecticide. Mealy bugs can be controlled with insecticidal soaps, or a strong jet stream of water. Malathion can be used, but should be saved as a last "nuclear" option. There is a systemic insecticide that can be used on Citrus trees in the ground, it is NOT labeled for container grown Citrus…yet. Please follow all label directions. The label is the law!

Citrus Rust Mite Damage

Spider Mite Damage

SPIDER & RUST MITES are tiny red or orange arachnids that also feed on plant juices. Spider mites can reproduce very quickly. Yellow or orange speckles on the leaves can be evidence that you have spider mites. They can be controlled with horticultural neem oil. If you use a type of pesticide, make sure the label reads for use on spider mites or is a miticide. Because they are arachnids, certain insecticides do not affect spider mites. If you are unsure if you have spider mites, take a plain piece of white paper and place it under the suspected leaves. Now tap the leaves rather sharply and look at the paper. If there are little dots moving around, you have spider mites.

Aphids on Citrus

APHIDS are another type of sucking insects. They like young new growth and can severely damage that growth in the spring. Aphids are usually in the presence of ants. They get along with each other in a loving way. Ants feed on the sticky honeydew that aphids produce and ants protect and help move the aphids around. Introducing ladybugs to the area will go along way in controlling this pest. Insecticidal soap will also help.

Citrus Leafminer (Adult)

Citrus Leafminer (Larvae)

Citrus Leafminer Damage-Both Pictures

   CITRUS LEAF MINERS are a recent introduction to the United States. CLM's are a nocturnal moth that lay their eggs on the undersides of young flushes of growth. After hatching in 4-5 days, the larvae begin tunneling just underneath the leaf surface, creating a squiggly pattern on the leaf. Once in the leaf, the miner is impossible to control. Horticultural oil seems to help in discouraging the moth from laying her eggs. Make sure you spray the undersides; she does not like the oily surface and will go elsewhere to lay the eggs. The problem here is, the plant itself is protecting the very pest that is eating it. This insect is more of a cosmetic damage problem, though the hole it leaves when leaving the leaf can be an entrance for Citrus diseases.

Whitefly

WHITEFLY is particularly bothersome because the damage they cause shows up long after they are gone. They live and breed on the undersides of leaves and feed on the juices of the leaves. You can tell you have Whitefly when, if you brush against the leaves and a white cloud like disturbance floats up, you have them. Insecticidal soap seems to be the best defense.

Orange Dog Larvae

ORANGE DOGS are leaf-chewing pests. They are the larvae of the Swallowtail Butterfly that you first met at the very beginning of this chapter. They are really kind of gross looking, as you see above. These pests can defoliate a young citrus tree in a matter of days if not hours. BT can be used to control this caterpillar, as well as just picking them off by hand.

GRASSHOPPERS as you can see, this pest loves to eat citrus leaves too. Any insecticide labeled for grasshoppers and citrus can be used for them. Hand picking is effective. Attracting birds will help also.

Bird Damage on Grapefruit

BIRDS can actually be beneficial and a nuisance. Usually it is the Mocking Birds that are the culprit. There have been many years that I have had this happen to my grapefruits and oranges. The birds literally just sit there and peck at the fruit, it swings out, and then back and they peck at it again. I thought maybe there was an insect issue, but there was nothing there. I honestly believe they are just playing with a "toy". It usually just makes the fruit ugly and does not affect the fruit taste. Other than a cat/dog or a bazooka, I have yet to find an effective deterrent. Please don't use the old CD on a string trick, especially if it is a Justin Beiber one, they will just read the label and laugh at you. One, because they know that trick and two, because you have a Justin Beiber cd!

That is not all of the pests that you may encounter, but it is probably the majority of the ones you will see on the wanted poster at the Post Office. Having a healthy ecosystem and creating habitats for beneficial insects, such as Ladybugs, Lacewings and Assassin Bugs will go a long way in keeping your pest population in check. If you do need to reach for a bottle of something, always follow the label on whatever you use. Start off with the least toxic product you can, often times that will be all you need. If after several attempts with different things, I usually save the big guns, Malathion, as the "Nuclear Option". If that doesn't work, which it has never failed me, I might consider a REAL nuclear option. Hopefully, none of us will ever have to rely on that!

How To Grow Citrus Practically Anywhere

If you see this over North Charleston, SC….everybody will be saying:

"Uh, Oh, Darren must have been having a major pest problem this year"

How To Grow Citrus Practically Anywhere

Citrus Black Spot

CHAPTER 10 Diseases

    Luckily, and comparatively speaking, citrus have the least amount of disease problems. If you compare them to, apples or peaches, citrus are the least problematic.

Now that is not to say they are trouble free, far from it. Citrus does have its share of problems.

    Florida and the quarantines (I will have a very in depth discussion on quarantines later) associated with that state would show that to be true. They have, Citrus Canker, Sweet Orange Scab and the biggest threat to the citrus industry, Citrus Greening. I will discuss each of these and a few others in this chapter. Depending on where you live and where you get your citrus tree from, you may or may not have to deal with any of these "biggies" as I will call them.

Citrus Canker is a bacterial disease that affects most types of citrus. While it is not harmful to humans, canker can affect the vitality of citrus trees, causing leaves and fruit to drop prematurely; a fruit infected with canker is safe to eat, but is too unsightly to be sold. Don't these just look yummy?

Infected fruit can be used for the processing of juice, just not in the fresh market.

Infection causes lesions or cankers to appear on the stems, leaves and fruit of citrus, including lemons, limes, grapefruit and oranges. Calamondins and Kumquats seem to be highly resistant to it. Mandarins and Citrons have a slightly lesser resistance, but are still moderately so. The lesions will be raised, brown, water-soaked margins, usually with a yellow halo or ring effect around it. Older lesions have a corky appearance, still in many cases retaining the halo effect. Once a grove is infected, it is very persistent. Citrus canker outbreaks are prevented and managed in a number of ways. In countries that do not have canker, the disease is prevented from entering the country by quarantine measures. In countries with new outbreaks, eradication programs started immediately after the disease has been discovered have proven to be successful; these programs rely on the destruction of affected groves.

When the eradication has been unsuccessful and the disease has become established, some options include replacing susceptible citrus cultivars with resistant ones, applying preventive sprays of a copper based bactericide, and destroying the infected trees and all surrounding trees within a certain radius.

In January 2000, the Florida Department of Agriculture adopted a policy of removing all infected trees and all citrus trees within a 1900-ft radius of an infected tree in both residential areas and commercial groves. Previous to this eradication policy, the department eradicated all citrus trees within 125 ft of an infected one. The program ended in January 2006 following a statement from the USDA that eradication was not feasible.

Sweet Orange Scab, another nasty disease, is a fungal one that mainly affects the rind of citrus. It results in unsightly scab like appearances on the outside of the fruit, less often on the twigs and leaves. It does not affect the internal flesh.

This disease will more commonly cause the fruit to drop prematurely and the scabby lesions will make the fruit unsalable in the fresh fruit market.

The fungus is easily spread by rain or irrigation and can be carried on other already infected plants and fruits. Insects can also spread the fungus when carrying fungal spores on their bodies. The pathogen survives between crops in pustules on infected leaves, twigs and fruit left on the tree. Sanitation is critical here in helping to break the cycle.

As long as there is sufficient moisture the disease can develop quite rapidly (in less than four hours) under optimum conditions (75-80 degrees). The first detection in the United States occurred on July 23, 2010 in Spring, Texas, near Houston on residential lemon and tangerine trees. As of this writing, it has now been confirmed in Louisiana, Florida, and most recently, Arizona. It can be controlled with a series of well-timed fungicide applications Sweet oranges and tangerines (including their hybrids) are most susceptible.

I could write an entire chapter on the next disease, it truly is the most devastating disease of citrus trees. It was first discovered in Florida in 2005, and at the time, they did not expect the citrus industry to survive more than another 10 years!

Citrus Greening, also known as Huanglongbing or HLB. It poses no harm or threat to humans or animals; it has destroyed millions of acres of crops. Once a tree is infected, there is no cure, as of the writing of this book.

This disease is so named because of the misshapen, non-ripening fruit the tree will produce. More times than not, the fruit will drop prematurely, the seeds inside will abort and the fruit will have a bitter taste to it. The tree will eventually succumb and die within a few years. Early signs of infection are, yellow mottled leaves, which incidentally mimics nutritional deficiencies such as those of zinc, iron, and manganese. Premature defoliation, twig dieback, decay of roots and lack of vigor are also indications.

It lives in the phloem tissue, which is the system that takes the food from the leaves and sends it to the rest of the plant. Like the human blood vessels, a blockage of these "arteries" by any foreign substance, can have dire effects.

The Asian Citrus Psyllid is the main vector in spreading this disease. This insect is no bigger than the head of a pin. It spreads the disease as it feeds on the leaves and stems of citrus trees. Once the Asian citrus psyllid picks up the disease, it carries it for the rest of its life. Grafting with a diseased scion or rootstock can also spread it.

Now before you freak out and think your tree has, remember I said it mimics some nutritional problems. If you have the slightest doubt that your tree has not been fed properly, go with that first.

Second, look at the leaves and see if they are blotched. Do you remember the old inkblot test? The one that you folded the paper in half and you had to describe what the image looked like when you unfolded it. Do that with your leaves.

Look at this picture of healthy leaves compared to leaves showing greening disease.

Did you notice how the infected leaves are not a mirror image of each side of the midrib? Again, that is no guarantee that you have the disease, but it could be another hint.

If you have all of the symptoms that I have mentioned above, or even if you just want piece of mind, please do not hesitate to send me some pictures of your tree. My e-mail is TheCitrusGuy@netzero.com. I will gladly check them out and let you know what I think is going on and give you some options.

Among the many, many wonderful websites out there on this serious problem, The Ministry of Agriculture and Fisheries down in Jamaica has this wonderful poster of what to look for if you suspect Citrus Greening.

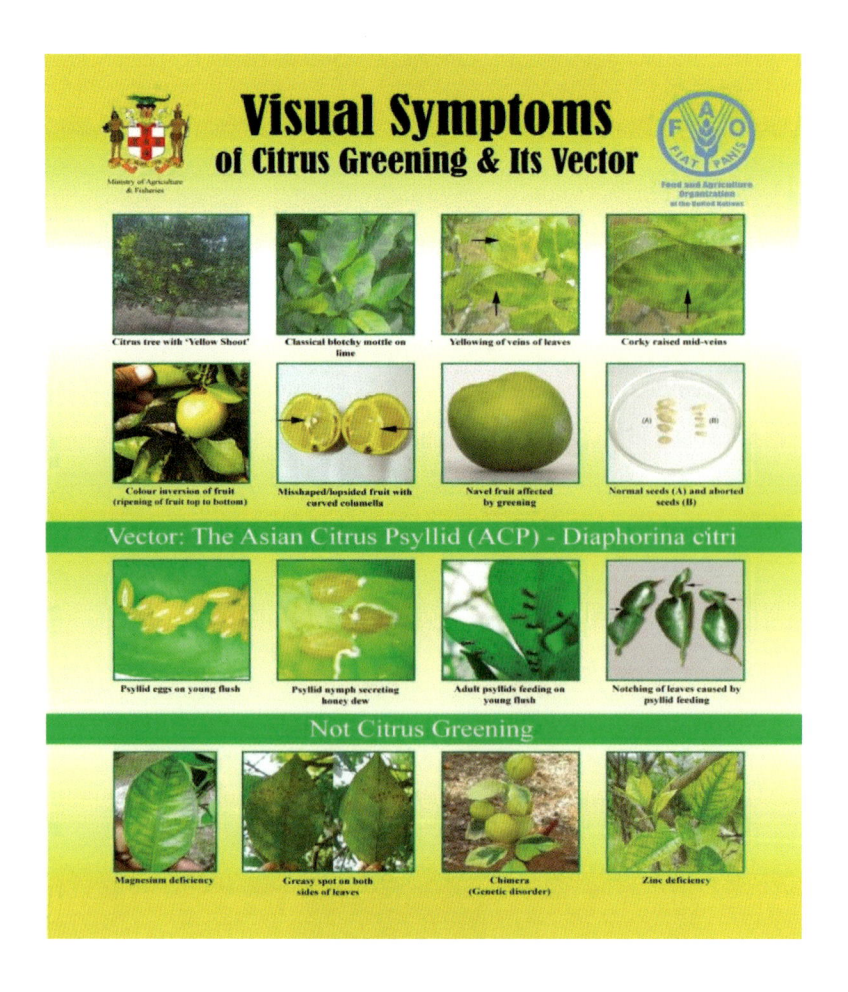

If it is too small to see here, their website is:
http://www.moa.gov.jm/PlantHealth/data/Symptoms%20Poster.jpg

I would strongly encourage you to research more on this disease; it really is crucial not to continue it's spread. As I mentioned at the beginning of this discussion, I could write an entire chapter on just this problem alone. During my lectures, I usually try to devote at least 15-20 minutes on it.

Another fantastic website to research about Citrus Greening is:
http://www.saveourcitrus.org/

This will give you almost everything you will need to know about, why there is quarantines, what the disease is, where it is, and much more! Please check it out and pass it along.

As for any other diseases, there are more, but usually not common. They tend to appear more in Citrus producing states and countries, where there are huge numbers of trees. Unless you pick up a tree that has a dormant disease in it, there should not be any worry. Always remember to buy from reputable nurseries and don't be afraid to ask questions and in some instances, check the roots by gently pulling the plant out of the pot.

We discussed the big ones, if you are uncertain that you may have a problem, do not hesitate to send me a picture, or five. I will help you as much as I can. TheCitrusGuy@netzero.com

Now, for a little test. Didn't see that one coming did you?

One of these pictures is Citrus Greening, one is Iron deficiency, and one is Magnesium Deficiency can you tell which is which?

If you knew the one on the top was Iron Deficiency, give yourself a Gold Star! The one in the middle is Citrus Greening. The bottom one is the Magnesium Deficiency. See how hard it is to tell the difference?

Imagine trying to detect it out in a grove of a thousand trees?

How To Grow Citrus Practically Anywhere

Citrus Leaf Sunburn

CHAPTER 11 Other Problems

After reading all of the pests and disease problems, the last thing you probably want to hear is another list of things that can go wrong. The good thing is, most of these are not horrible, but can possibly happen. Most of these do not fit into pests or diseases, so I decided to have this chapter.

The first problem I would like to discuss is dry fruit.

I know, it sounds pretty self-explanatory, I pick a fruit and it is dry. But why does this happen?

There actually can be several reasons. The first one will make you go, duh!

Lack of water. If the tree is not receiving enough moisture, it will literally rob the fruit of its moisture, so the tree will survive. It is a preservation technique. So, the best way to fix this is, of course, make sure the tree is always properly irrigated.

Another reason is, if the fruit has been left on the tree too long. Citrus have a certain life expectancy. If that time has elapsed, the fruit start to break down. The moisture is re-absorbed to the tree and, hence, dries out.

Infancy can also cause this problem. If the tree is very young and been grown from a seed, the fruit can be dry. The only way to alleviate this problem is to allow the tree to mature. Give it another year, or possibly two, for it to get older, this problem should just go away. Interestingly enough, infancy in a young, seed grown tree can also have the reverse affect. You may get some fruit that is very bland and watery tasting. Same situation, allow some years to gain maturity and the blandness will go away.

I would like to emphasize here, the importance of moisture levels (Chapter 7) in your citrus tree. Especially if you are going to grow them in containers, which I am assuming you wanted to do in the first place, you are reading this book!

In the past, I have had problems with citrus splitting. My Republic of Texas orange seemed to be the most susceptible. The fruit would literally split open and reveal the innards, allowing it to spoil and become inedible, as you can see in the next picture.

Splitting is what is known as an Abiotic Disorder. That is a disorder that cannot be attributed to any living organism, such as an insect or pathogen, but happens because of an environmental or cultural condition. The reason that this was happening was due to a sudden intake of moisture. If the tree is not kept at a constant level of moisture and allowed to dry out too much between each watering, when it does get a drink of water, the fruit tries to absorb it all at once. The cells of the fruit cannot expand fast enough to absorb all of this new water and it splits. Fruit on young trees are more prone to fruit splitting than fruit on older trees, probably because there is more tree to absorb the excess water.

This situation is very disheartening, not only does it waste the fruit; it creates a good breeding ground for fruit flies and attracts other insect pests. The split fruit should be removed as soon as it is found and discarded as it may also harbor fungi or other bacteria.
The split fruit is edible, however most of the time it is not ripe enough to be usable.

There are also nutritional deficiencies that can be associated with this problem. While improper fertilization does not cause fruit splitting, low potassium levels can cause fruit peels to become thin and more prone to this phenomenon.

Chimeras. What is a chimera? They can actually be kind of cool, not necessarily a problem. Chimeras are the result of a mutation, which is present in some cells and not in others. This mutation occurs in a meristem (an area of active growth and division), and is replicated by normal cell division, creating parts of the plant with different genetic constitutions. Plant tissues are produced in distinct layers, and some of the most common plant chimeras are the result of a mutation in one of these layers. Layman's terms….it makes the fruit funky, either with variegation or very strange growths! Here are a few examples of Citrus Chimeras.

There is not much you can do about it, and there is nothing to worry about, the fruit is still very much edible. I find them very interesting.

Did you see the picture at the very top of this chapter of some sunburned citrus leaves? This can VERY easily happen to those of us that grow citrus in containers, especially those in the colder areas that need to protect them during the winter.

This is the scenario. Winter arrives and you bring your plant in to protect it. Even if you have it in a place where it gets lots of sun, it will never be the same as outdoors. This includes having grow lights on it. It may drop many of the leaves it has, or, the leaves will start to get accustomed to the darker conditions. All is well, the cold did not kill it, and it is still alive. Spring shows up and you can't wait to get your tree back outside because you know it suffered over the winter. It only takes two or three days and suddenly all of the leaves are looking faded, bleached or burnt and discolored. This is sunburn. The rays of the sun were too much for the tender, dark accustomed leaves. It won't kill the tree, but it will stunt it slightly.

This can happen if you lose a large tree or limb that may have been giving it some late afternoon shade too.

How do you avoid all of this?

It is actually quite easy. When it is time to bring your plant back to the great outdoors, do so slowly. Maybe you can put in under a tree so it only gets an hour or so of direct sun. After 3-4 days, move it so it gets a few more hours. You will want to continue this for about two weeks. By then, hopefully, it will be readjusted to the full sun it desires.

This can also happen to the fruit.

As a final note on sunburn, you can try applying an SPF 15 or higher on it, but I doubt it will work. It may actually intensify the effects of the sun. If the folks at Coppertone or Hawaiian Tropic are reading this, I just gave you an idea for a new product. Let me know, I will gladly test it for you

How To Grow Citrus Practically Anywhere

Anyone can count the seeds in a lemon, but only God can count the number of lemons in a seed.

> By Darren Sheriff with my apologies to Robert H. Schuller

CHAPTER 12 Reproduction/Propagation

At one time, I had well over 100 different cultivars of citrus growing in my yard. Yes, they were all in containers.

Usually the first question that I was asked was, 'Where did you get all of them?"

Everywhere was my usual response.

I have many friends that grow citrus. The Internet was mainly to blame for my outlandish collection. It is increasingly dangerous to get seeds from some of the places that I did. Quarantines, new diseases, and increasing rates of established diseases make it far less attractive to import seeds. Cuttings from abroad are a definite No-No! Even cuttings from quarantine areas are taboo. I should add in here that I have since reduced the number of trees that I have. As of the writing of this book, I am sitting right around 65 varieties.

Okay, that still doesn't answer where I got them, or how I got them to grow. If you are looking for grafting tips, stop reading right here. I have attempted grafting citrus, while I know it can be done, I can't seem to get the hang of it. There are many websites out there that will show you how to graft; I encourage you to look some of them up. I know it just takes practice; time is not always on my side.

Rooting cuttings is possible, but definitely falls under the "a tad bit harder than some things" category.

The gist of rooting cuttings is about the same as Camellias. The cuttings should be taken in mid- to late summer into early fall. The cuttings should be between 6 and 8 inches long. Depending on what you are trying to root will depend on how long it takes.

The procedure goes like this. You want to get cuttings from the current year's growth that has partially hardened or ripened. Remove all but two of the leaves and cut the remaining leaves on the cutting in half to reduce moisture loss. You may also want to strip the bark about one half inch up each side from the cut end, this will help induce rooting.

Use a soilless mixture such as peat or bark with a little perlite thrown in. Dip the root end in the rooting hormone. There are many available out there, use the one you are most familiar with. I prefer Root-Gel by

Dyno-Gro, it is much better than powder, which will actually wick moisture from the cutting. In my opinion, it is also better than liquid that will not stay on the cutting. The gel sticks and insulates the cutting until it develops roots.

Using a pencil make a hole in the medium approximately 3-4 inches deep. Insert the cutting deep enough for it to be able to stand upright. Firm the soil around the stem and water gently to settle the cutting. Make Sure You Label It!! I promise, you WILL forget what the cutting is.

Keep the cutting humid. Give it some bottom heat of 64-70 degrees if you can, this will speed up the rooting process. Misting the cuttings occasionally will also help. Keep the medium moist, not wet, like a wrung out damp dish sponge.

Another good tip that I picked up some time ago is to use clear plastic cups or soda bottles. You will be able to see the roots instead of pulling on the cutting occasionally to see if they have taken. You run the risk of ripping the roots out before they even have a chance to get a good hold.

As for how long it takes to get them to root? Like I said earlier, depends on what it is.

For example, Lemons, limes and citrons should root readily within 4 to 6 weeks.

Sweet oranges, sour oranges, grapefruit, trifoliate orange and citranges are intermediate, rooting with 6 to 8 weeks. Mandarins are considered to be the most difficult to root and may take up to 16 weeks.

This is what you are striving for in regards to what the cuttings should look like.

If they start to flower before they root, as in the above picture, trim off the buds. That will allow the energy to go to the rooting process.

Air layering is similar to rooting the cuttings. The difference here is, the cutting does not get taken off of the tree until it has actually formed roots.

To use this method, start with a small limb, approximately 12 to 15 inches from the tip of the twig. Make two parallel, very shallow cuts, just through the bark about three quarters to one inch apart, all of the way around the limb. Then, make a cut within that band you just created, extending from one side to the other. To remove the band of bark, use a pair of pliers, gently, gripping the band of bark and twisting it off. Scrape off any green cambium left behind when the bark peels off. Pure white wood is what we are after.

You can speed up the rooting process by dusting hormone powder on the exposed area, but, like I said above, powder wicks moisture. I prefer using the sphagnum moss that has been soaked in a little bit of liquid hormone. Wrap the exposed section of the limb with the moist sphagnum peat moss and hold it in place with plastic wrap. Then place some aluminum foil around that, shiny side down. The reason you want to put the shiny side down is, it will not be as attractive to squirrels and birds. You can also spray a little dark green or tan paint on it, to make it a little less obtrusive looking.

    This is one of the best pictures I have seen to give you a better idea of what this whole process looks like.

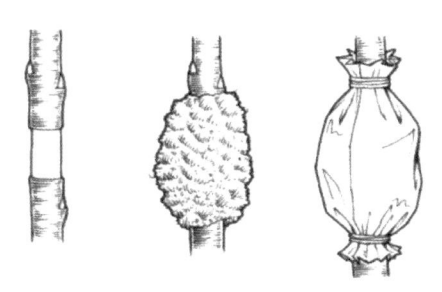

    After about two months, give the "potato" a light squeeze; if it feels rather hard, there are roots in there. Cut the limb below the rooted area and plant the limb, with the foil/plastic wrap removed, but the sphagnum moss still attached, in a container filled with potting mix. Water the plant and keep it in a shady, humid location until roots begin to fill the pot.

    This method works great if you want to multiply the plants you already have or have a friend that does not mind the air layering being on their tree.

    Personally, I find growing citrus from seed the easiest and cheapest of all. Again, depending on what you want to grow, will determine how long it will take to produce fruit.

WARNING!!

Patience is most definitely a prerequisite, especially when it comes to planting citrus from seed. This whole process can take anywhere from 2-10 years to actually get fruit.

Key Limes and Calamondins are the quickest, fruiting in about 2-3 years. I have actually gotten a Lemonquat to fruit in 18 months from seed, though I think I just lucked out there. Oranges, Lemons, Limes and Mandarins fall in the 5-7 years time frame. Grapefruit is usually the longest, 8-10 even up to 12 years. These time frames are relative! They depend on how well you take care of them. If given the proper sunlight, water, fertilizer and warmth/protection, you can be on the lower end of these times. If you are a little lax in your horticulture practices, of course, it will take longer.

As for being cheap, go to your grocery store or get some fruit from a friend. As long as there are seeds, it will produce fruit. There is some controversy over whether or not it will come true to type. The chances are YES! Even if not, you may get something as good as the fruit you just ate, not quite as good as or something even better!

2 out of 3 isn't bad! You will definitely get fruit.

Over the years, I have learned and figured out a good way to get the seeds to germinate better. My thought process went like this. The fruit, full of seeds, falls to the ground. There, it decays and the seeds lay on top of the soil. They germinate and produce more plants/trees. Why then, do we insist on burying the seeds when we plant them? Mother Nature has this figured out, why do we mess with it?

So, I started just pressing the seeds into the top of the soil. Your favorite potting soil is fine; there is no secret concoction that will be better than another. I keep them warm and moist. My germination rate is about 99% as opposed to 50% or less when I actually "planted" the seeds.

Give it a try and see how much better it works for you.

How To Grow Citrus Practically Anywhere

How To Grow Citrus Practically Anywhere

"If you wish to make anything grow, you must understand it, and understand it in a very real sense. 'Green fingers' are a fact, and a mystery only to the unpracticed. But green fingers are the extensions of a verdant heart."
— **Russell Page**, **The Education of a Gardener**

CHAPTER 13: A Tidy Little Summary

   Well then, there you have it. You now have an understanding, and description, on how you can grow citrus practically anywhere. Knowledge is power and understanding how things grow is the greatest of plant knowledge.

   We have discussed history, what to grow them in, water, fertilizers and sunlight.

You know what kind of problems to look out for, be it, diseases, insects or some other entity that may attack your precious plants.

Even with quarantines in place, you know how to propagate plants. Please make sure you abide by the quarantines! They are in place for a reason and I have put way too much blood, sweat and tears into my collection for it to all go to garbage because somebody bought and transported a plant illegally.

We have gone into every nook and cranny that I can possibly think of, to assist you in creating a hospitable environment for your new hobby.

I wish you all of the luck in the world, and hope for your success in growing at least a little "citrusy" fruit. You may never have enough fruit to start a farmer's market, but just think of how good it will feel to pour yourself a glass of Orange Juice from the fruit you picked this morning or slice a wedge of Lemon from your backyard for that glass of iced tea, that you grew!

What was that? I should mention a few places that you CAN get trees legally?! Well then, sit right down for a few more minutes; let's see what we can come up with.

Back in the Preface, I mentioned my friend, Stan McKenzie. He is in the Lake City, SC area. I have known "Stan, The Citrus Man" for many years and have bought a fair number of trees from him. If you would like to visit his website, go to http://mckenzie-farms.com/. He will treat you right! Let him know where you saw his name and page.

Another nursery in South Carolina that has some good, cold hardy type of citrus is in Aiken, SC. Their website is http://www.woodlanders.net/. Check them out.

One last place I will tell you about is out in California. I have not personally bought anything from them, but I have heard nothing but good things about their trees. To visit the website go to https://www.fourwindsgrowers.com/index.php.

If you live in the Charleston, SC area, I invite you to join the Lowcountry Fruit Growers Society. There, you will meet lots of fruit enthusiast and will be able to share seeds and plants with them. A website for that group is http://lowcountryfruit.blogspot.com/p/about_5166.html.

The main reason that the LFGS is in existence is because of the California Rare Fruit Growers Society. I started the Lowcountry group because we didn't have anything like that here on the east coast. The California group is great and I encourage you to join them if you are out that way. http://www.crfg.org/.

As a final website to visit, pertaining to fruit, is the Southern Fruit Fellowship. There are a lot of great people involved in that group and is another on my list to check out. https://southernfruitfellowship.wordpress.com/about/.

Lastly, the nursery that I currently work at, Hidden Ponds Nursery, sells citrus. Their website is http://www.hiddenpondsnursery.com/. You can learn all about them, the animals on the premises and get directions to visit.

Well, that will keep you busy on the web, looking for citrus trees. If you ever have any problems, questions, or just run into something that you are not sure about, I am only an e-mail away…..TheCitrusGuy@netzero.com

How To Grow Citrus Practically Anywhere

CHAPTER 14: What to do with it, once you grow it

There are probably a million recipes that you can find online to use your new hobbies produce. Everything from salads and appetizers, to main courses and desserts, you just have to do a little Google search.

I was going to list a few recipes here, but decided just to give a few tips and tricks on things you may not have really thought of.

I am NOT a big fan of marmalade, made the traditional way with Seville Oranges. However, when it is made with Kumquats with or without Habanera Peppers, then you have something I really like.

Served as a glaze over chicken or pork as a main dish or with cream cheese and crackers as a snack, it is definitely worth a try.

If you have a favorite Lemon Meringue recipe, substitute the lemon with lime, kumquat, calamondin or any other citrus for a killer dessert. I have also done the same substituting with a favorite cheesecake recipe. You will want to play around with the amounts of citrus juice you put in it, some are a little stronger and/or sweeter than others.

You can add some shredded zest from any of the citrus to your favorite sugar cookie recipe. Just think of a key lime or maybe a grapefruit enhanced sugar cookie.

If you get enough different fruits, even a simple mixed citrus fruit salad with cottage cheese is a fantastic, low calorie snack.

The biggest thing I want you to get from this chapter is, don't be afraid to experiment! Think outside the box. Citrus fruit is something that pairs nicely with so many other things. Pomegranate and orange muffins, or Blueberry muffins with a lemon glaze may not sound great at first, but trust me, they work!

How about an orange zest and bread crumb chicken breast? Or lemon/lime chicken tenderloins with some scalloped potatoes? Hungry yet?

My final food for thought, I haven't tried this one yet, but it really sounds good, candied orange peel brownies. You take your brownie recipe, add some dark chocolate chips and some candied orange peel. There are recipes on line that show you how to candy the peel.

I truly hope you will add some of these ideas to your cooking repertoire, and experiment with making some new meals of your own. It has been a pleasure writing this book, I hope you have enjoyed reading it. Please drop me a line sometime and let me know what you thought! TheCitrusGuy@netzero.com

Watch for more of my writings coming out in the future!

Happy Growing!

How To Grow Citrus Practically Anywhere

About The Author:

Darren Sheriff is a Certified Professional Nurseryman, a Charleston County Master Gardener and he works for Terra Bella Garden Center in North Charleston, South Carolina. He is known as "The Citrus Guy" and has more than 65 different varieties of citrus in his yard, all in containers. Darren is the founder and current President of the Lowcountry Fruit Growers Society as well as the current President of the Coastal Carolina Camellia Society. Recently becoming an accredited Camellia Flower judge, he judges and competes all throughout much of the southeast. He loves education and teaching, so he started a gardening blog to help extend that mission. It is not only educational but also sometimes funny and hopefully always inspirational. It can be found at http://thecitrusguy.blogspot.com/.

His website is http://thecitrusguy.com/

He loves helping people with their garden problems. Look him up on Facebook as The Citrus Guy or you can contact him at TheCitrusGuy@netzero.com for your questions about this book, your garden, or pretty much anything relating to the horticultural world.

Printed in Great Britain
by Amazon